# PLANNING A RICH LIFE BY 30

*A Millennial's Guide to Financial Independence*

## EVAN M. DANE

*Evan M. Dane*

*"Pay attention to the small things in the world that make life richer and more satisfying."*

-Carl Hilty

*"He that is of the opinion money will do everything may well be suspected of doing everything for money."*

-Benjamin Franklin

*"When the last tree is cut down, the last fish eaten and the last stream poisoned, you will realize that you cannot eat money."*

-Michael Ende

To the young ones who want to be
financially stable and rich by 30 to avoid
financial embarrassment.

*Evan M. Dane*

Table of Content

# Part I

# Laying the Foundation for Financial Independence

# Introduction to Financial Independence

**M**illennials have a unique opportunity to shape their financial futures because of the unprecedented access to information and resources that comes with living in the digital age. The goal of becoming financially independent, or what many like to refer to as "rich by 30," is not just a pipe dream for a small group of people; it can become a reality for those who are prepared to set out on a path of self-discovery, financial education, and methodical planning.

### *The Dream of Economic Freedom*

Imagine living a life free from financial restrictions, where your income serves as a tool to help you achieve your goals rather than being used only to pay bills and debt.

Being financially independent means having the freedom to pursue your passions and values without being constrained by the need to accumulate wealth. It's the freedom to follow your passions, see the world, donate to causes you believe in, and spend time with the people you care about without worrying about how much money you make.

## *Achievable Goal Setting*

Establishing attainable goals and a clear vision are the first steps on the path to financial independence. It's more important to make gradual progress in the direction of your ideal degree of financial independence and comfort than it is to suddenly accumulate enormous wealth. Whether your financial goals are to start a business, travel the world, retire early, or just have financial peace of mind, we'll go over the steps you need to take in this chapter to define them.

## *A Self-Dedication*

You will require discipline, commitment, and a readiness to change and grow if you choose to go on this adventure. It takes a personal commitment to become financially independent, a pledge you make to yourself to put your financial health first. It's about controlling your financial future instead of allowing external factors to determine your financial fate.

## What This Book Is About to Give

We'll explore a variety of topics related to reaching financial independence in the next chapters. We'll go over the value of financial literacy, the fundamentals of saving and budgeting, career advancement tactics, and the potential of investing. We'll talk about starting your own business and how it can help you with your financial goals. We'll talk about risk management, the value of keeping an optimistic outlook, and long-term financial planning. We'll also exchange tools and resources to support you along the way. Being financially independent is a way of life, not just a destination. It all comes down to making wise financial decisions and keeping an optimistic outlook that is in line with your goals. Although it's not always simple, it is definitely attainable.

*Key Takeaways*

Millennials who are prepared to take charge of their financial future can achieve financial independence.

One of the most important first steps toward financial independence is setting attainable goals.

The path to financial independence requires dedication, self-control, and education.

# Financial Literacy Essentials

I n the digital age, information is widely available, but many people still struggle to acquire financial literacy, a crucial type of knowledge. This chapter delves deeply into the subject, examining the critical significance of financial literacy and offering helpful tools to increase your understanding of money matters.

More than just a catchphrase, financial literacy serves as the cornerstone of your financial independence. The ability to successfully understand and manage your finances is the fundamental component of financial literacy. It covers a wide range of information, from fundamentals of finance to more advanced subjects like investing and retirement planning.

*What makes financial literacy so important?*

Imagine attempting to cross a large ocean without any navigational experience or star guidance. In a similar vein, attempting to make sense of the complicated financial world without having sufficient financial literacy can result in uncertainty, bad financial choices, and lost opportunities. Knowing finances gives you the ability to:

**1. Make Well-Informed Decisions:** Having financial literacy enables you to plan for the future, save, invest, and budget your money with knowledge.

**2. Safeguard Your Resources**: Gaining an understanding of financial concepts such as risk, insurance, and investments can help safeguard your acquired wealth and reduce potential losses.

**3. Create Richness:** Equipped with a solid understanding of finance, you can spot chances to increase your wealth through business ventures, investments, and other sources of revenue.

**Fundamental Financial Ideas**

It's crucial to understand the following fundamental financial concepts before delving into the intricacies of personal finance:

- **Income**: Your total earnings, which comprise your pay, salary, and any additional sources of income.

- **Expenses**: The cash you spend on a range of necessities and desires, such as groceries, entertainment, bills, and other items.

- **Budgeting**: The process of keeping tabs on your earnings and out-of-pocket costs to make sure you don't spend more than you make.

- **Saving**: Saving a portion of your earnings for unforeseen expenses or future needs.

- **Debt**: Amounts owed to lenders, including loans and credit card debt.

- **Investing**: Putting money down to purchase assets that you hope will increase in value or produce income over time.

## Sources to Increase Your Financial Literacy

When it comes to achieving financial literacy, you're not alone. The following are some excellent resources to aid in your financial education:

**1. Bookstore:** Several books written by authorities in the field are available on investing and personal finance. These books can offer in-depth analysis on a range of financial subjects.

**2. Online Programs:** Numerous websites provide low-cost or free financial literacy courses. Personal finance courses are available on websites such as Coursera, Udemy, and Khan Academy.

**3. Podcasts and Blogs about Finance:** Numerous podcasts and blogs are devoted to money management and financial education. You can gain knowledge from the insights and counsel of successful people and financial experts.

**4. Financial Advisors:** For individualized advice, think about speaking with a financial advisor. They can offer you specialized guidance and assist you in developing a financial plan.

Being financially literate is a lifelong process that requires constant learning and adjustment. You're making a significant step toward financial independence by investing time in increasing your financial literacy.

The foundation of financial independence is financial literacy.

Financial literacy is based on fundamental financial ideas such as income, expenses, budgeting, saving, debt, and investing.

You can easily expand your financial knowledge by using readily available resources like books, online courses, blogs, podcasts, and financial advisors.

# Setting Financial Goals

T o embark on your journey towards financial independence, you must set clear, realistic, and actionable financial goals. Goals serve as your roadmap, guiding your financial decisions and actions. In this chapter, we will explore the process of setting financial goals and provide guidance on turning them into attainable milestones.

### *The Power of Setting Goals*

Goals are not merely wishes; they are the compass that points you in the right direction. They give you a sense of purpose and motivation to work toward a better financial future. Whether your goal is to buy a home, pay off student loans, start a business, travel the world, or retire early, defining your objectives is the first step towards making your dreams a reality.

### Guidelines for Setting Financial Goals

**1. Be Specific:** Your goals should be clear and well-defined. Instead of saying, "I want to save money," specify the amount you wish to save and the purpose of the savings. For example, "I want to save $5,000 for a down payment on a house."

2. **Make Them Measurable:** Your goals should be quantifiable so that you can track your progress. Define how you will measure success. For instance, "I will save $500 per month to reach my goal of $10,000 in 20 months."

3. **Set Realistic Targets:** While it's crucial to aim high, your goals should also be attainable within your current financial situation. Setting unattainable goals can be demotivating. Ensure your goals align with your income, expenses, and resources.

4. **Establish a Timeline:**Give yourself a deadline for achieving your goals. A timeframe adds urgency and commitment.

For example, "I will save $5,000 for a down payment in the next 10 months."

5. **Break Down Larger Goals:** If your primary goal seems overwhelming, break it down into smaller, more manageable sub-goals.

**Types of Financial Goals**

There are different types of financial goals, each serving a specific purpose in your financial journey:

★ **1 Short-Term Goals:** These are goals that you aim to achieve within the next 1 to 2 years. Examples include Models incorporate making a backup stash, taking care of exorbitant interest obligation, or putting something aside for an excursion

★ 2 **Mid-Term Goals:** These goals typically have a timeframe of 3 to 5 years. Examples may include saving for a down payment on a home or starting a business.

★ **Long-Term Goals:** These are often your most significant financial aspirations, usually spanning over 5 years. Long-term goals might include saving for retirement, purchasing a second home, or building a substantial investment portfolio.

### *Turning Goals into Action*

Once you've defined your financial goals, it's time to turn them into actionable steps. Create a plan that outlines what you need to do to achieve each goal. This plan should include specifics such as how much you need to save each month, investment strategies, or actions required for debt reduction.

With clear goals and a well-defined plan, you're now equipped to make informed financial decisions that lead you closer to achieving your dreams. In the subsequent chapters, we'll delve into specific strategies to help you achieve your goals and pave the way to financial independence.

Clear, measurable, realistic, and time-bound goals are the foundation of your financial journey.

Short-term, mid-term, and long-term goals serve different purposes in your financial planning.

Transform your financial goals into actionable steps and plans to ensure steady progress toward financial independence.

It's critical to balance your short- and long-term goals when establishing your financial objectives. Reaching this balance can assist you in preserving your financial security as you strive toward a more promising and safe future.

## *The Significance of Short-term Objectives*

Short-term objectives provide you a feeling of rapid accomplishment and satisfaction. Usually, you can accomplish these objectives in the ensuing year or two. These can be setting up an emergency fund, eliminating high-interest debt, or accumulating money for a well-earned trip. The following benefits of short-term goals are available:

→ **Rapid Success:** Reaching short-term objectives can happen quite quickly and easily. These victories can help you stay motivated and confident while keeping you on course.

→ **De-stressing**: Reaching short-term objectives can improve your general well-being and lessen financial stress. For example, settling a high-interest credit card debt can result in a notable alleviation of financial strain.

→ **Adaptability:** When your circumstances change, you can more easily adapt and adjust short-term goals. They give you the freedom to take on unforeseen financial obstacles head-on.

### *The Strength of Long-term Objectives*

Long-term financial objectives usually cover a period of five years or more and look further into the future. Long-term objectives can be things like building significant wealth, buying a house, or saving for retirement. These objectives are equally important for a number of reasons:

1. **Wealth Accumulation**: Your main route to financial independence is through long-term objectives. You can gradually amass wealth by diversifying your investment portfolio or setting aside money for retirement.

2. **Security:** As you get older, long-term objectives provide financial security. For example, saving for retirement guarantees that you will have enough money to continue living the way you want in your later years.

3. **Building Legacy:** Leaving a financial legacy that helps not only you but also

future generations can be one of your long-term objectives. These objectives might include wealth generation and estate planning.

### *Short-Term and Long-Term Goal Balancing*

Planning and careful thought may be necessary to strike a balance between short- and long-term goals. Even though it can be tempting to only think about immediate financial relief, keeping a long-term outlook is just as important for safeguarding your financial future. Here's how to achieve that equilibrium:

1. **Prioritize Debt:** Since high-interest debt can impede the achievement of both short- and long-term objectives, start by taking

care of it. Getting rid of this debt is frequently a crucial short-term goal.

2. **Emergency Fund:** Concurrently, set up an emergency fund to deal with unforeseen costs. This reduces immediate stress and offers a safety net for finances.

3. **Make Future Investments:** As soon as you have paid off high-interest debt and established an emergency fund, you should start investing for your long-term financial goals. Over time, investments have the potential to increase significantly.

4. **Monthly Evaluation:** Make sure your financial objectives are still relevant and attainable by reviewing them from time to time. As your circumstances change, make adjustments to your long- and short-term goals.

In addition to ensuring that your immediate needs are met, balancing your short- and long-term financial goals also helps you secure a prosperous future.

## Building a Solid Foundation

E stablishing a strong financial foundation is an essential first step in the journey to financial independence. The two main pillars of financial stability that are covered in this chapter are saving and budgeting.

These habits help you make wise decisions and manage your money wisely, laying the foundation for your financial future.

### *The Value of Setting Up a Budget*

A budget is an effective tool that helps you take charge of your money, not a straitjacket. It functions as a road map to help you make financial decisions and make sure the money you spend is going toward your needs, objectives, and wants.

## A Budget-Creating Process

To generate a budget that works, adhere to these guidelines:

1. **Income Assessment:** To begin, figure out how much money you make each month from all of your sources of income, including wages, salary, and any additional sources.

2. **Expense Evaluation:** Divide your outgoings into non-essentials (such as eating out, entertainment, and subscriptions) and necessities (such as utilities, groceries, and rent or a mortgage).

3. **Determining Priorities:**Set aside a portion of your income to pay for necessities first. Next, set aside some for debt service and savings.

4. **Monitoring and Adjusting:**bKeep a close eye on your expenditures and make necessary adjustments. Make the required changes to make sure you don't go over your budget.

### The Ability to Save

Savings serve as a safety net for your money. They give you the financial buffer you need to deal with unforeseen costs and guarantee you're ready for new opportunities. Staying consistent is the key to successful saving.

**Savings Types**

- **Currency Reserve:** Establishing an emergency fund should be your first savings objective. In times of unforeseen financial difficulties, this fund can be a lifesaver and should cover three to six months' worth of living expenses.

- **Economic Reductions:** These are savings designated for particular, immediate objectives, like a trip, a down payment on a house, or a new vehicle.

- **Eternal Conserving:** These are intended to help you achieve your long-term financial goals, such as saving for retirement and gradually accumulating wealth.

## *The Rule of 50/30/20*

The 50/30/20 rule is a well-liked budgeting technique for allocating your income:

- ❖ **50% for necessities:** Set aside 50% of your income for necessities like housing, utilities, groceries, and transit.

❖ **30% for Non-Essentials:**Set aside 30% for expenses such as entertainment, dining out, and personal indulgences.

❖ **Set Aside 20% for Savings**: Set aside 20% for savings, covering emergency fund contributions, retirement savings, and other financial objectives.

**Application of This To implement saving and budgeting:**

a. **Create a Budget:**Assemble a budget that accounts for your earnings and outlays, emphasizing the need to balance necessary and discretionary spending.

b. **Automate Savings:** To make it simpler to consistently save each month, set up automatic transfers to your savings accounts.

c.**Reduce Unnecessary Expenses**: Determine which expenses are unnecessary for your financial objectives or well-being, and make the necessary cuts.

d. **Emergency Fund:** To provide you with financial stability and peace of mind, make emergency fund building a top priority.

You can build a solid financial foundation to support your journey toward financial independence by becoming an expert at budgeting and saving.

A strong financial base includes both an emergency fund and a responsible debt management strategy. These two factors can have a big impact on your path to financial independence and are your lifelines in difficult financial times.

**Establishing an Emergency Reserve**

**1. Aim Big, Start Small:** If you've never saved before, start small with a $500 or $1,000 savings target. Build up an emergency fund over time that can pay for three to six months' worth of living expenses.

**2. Automate Savings:**As soon as you get your paycheck, set up automatic transfers to your emergency fund to show that saving money is important. This guarantees steady contributions.

**3. Special Account:** Establish a different savings account specifically for your emergency fund. You can save money by not using this separation for non-emergencies.

**4. Use Windfalls Wisely**:To strengthen your emergency fund, allocate windfalls such as tax refunds, bonuses, or gifts directly to it. The emergency fund should not be used as a "rainy day" fund for non-essential items.

**5. Resist the Temptation.** Keep it only for true emergencies, such as unexpected job loss, auto repairs, or medical costs.

**Effective Debt Management**

1. **Give high-interest debt priority:** Repaying credit card debt and other high-interest debt should be your first priority. To save interest and pay off your debt more quickly, make larger than the minimum payments.

2. **Avalanche or Snowball of Debt:** Examine two well-liked approaches to paying off debt: the avalanche method

(paying off the highest interest debt first) and the snowball method (paying off the smallest debt first). Select the option that best fits your financial and psychological needs.

3. **Consolidate Debt**: To lower total interest payments, if you have several high-interest debts, think about combining them into a single loan with a lower interest rate or a credit card balance transfer.

4. **Discuss Interest Rates:** Make an effort to work out a lower interest rate with your creditors or ask for a lower-rate balance transfer. Reducing your interest rate can help you pay off debt much more quickly.

5. **Debt Repayment Budget**: Make debt payments a non-negotiable expense in your budget. Set aside a certain percentage of your monthly income to pay off debt.

6. **Remain on Course:** It's critical to continue consistent, disciplined debt repayment. To stay motivated, keep track of your progress and recognize your accomplishments.

7. **Avoid New Debt:** Take care not to take on new debt while you pay off your current debt. Refrain from taking out new loans or making more purchases with high-interest credit cards.

Recall that having an emergency fund reduces your financial stress and acts as a safety net. Both procedures are essential to laying a strong financial foundation.

# Part II

# Earning, Investing, and Entrepreneurship

# Earning Your Way to Financial Freedom

Your income is one of the biggest determinants on your path to financial independence. This chapter focuses on ways to boost your income, such as pursuing side projects, negotiating a raise, and professional development.

## *The Importance of Maximizing Your Income*

The engine that drives your financial journey is your income. Your ability to make more money gives you more chances to invest, save, and reach your financial objectives.

## Career Advancement Strategies

1. **Ongoing Education:** Invest on your education and experience. Keep up with developments in the field and look for chances to advance your career. Think about obtaining workshops, certifications, or courses that will improve your knowledge.

2. **Networking**: Attend industry events, join pertinent associations, and look for mentorship to help you develop a strong professional network. Professional guidance and possibilities might arise through networking.

3. **Seek Promotions:**Take the initiative to ask for changes in responsibility and promotions within your existing position. Advancement in your job may result from proving your worth to your employer.

4. **Assess Your Work Satisfaction**:Determine how satisfied you are with your job right now. If you're not happy, it might be time to look into other options that are more in line with your values and objectives.

**Pay Discussion**

1. **Examination**: Find out what the pay scale for your position and area is in the business. Recognize the value of your experience and talents in the employment market.

2. **Prepare**: Before pay talks, compile a summary of your achievements, competencies, and any extra benefits you provide to your company.

3. **Practice**: To gain confidence and successfully communicate your points, role-play the negotiation with a friend or mentor.

4. **Have Self-Assurance:** Retain faith in your value and your contributions throughout the negotiating process. Never accept less than you feel you are entitled to.

**Looking Into Side Projects**

➤ **Identify Your Skills**: Take into account your special abilities and interests, then look for ways to make money from them. Online sales of goods and services as well as freelancing are examples of side jobs.

➤ **Time Management:** Make effective use of your time. It's critical to strike a balance between your full-time job and your side project because side gigs can be taxing.

➤ **Initiate Little:** To test the waters, start your side project part-time. You can choose whether it's worth spending additional time and money on it as it expands.

➤ **Spread Your Revenue Streams:** Seek for several sources of extra money. In addition to stability, diversification may increase total earnings.

One of the most important things in reaching your financial objectives is your income. You're increasing your income potential by actively seeking career development, negotiating your pay, and investigating side gigs.

***Emphasizing the Value of Ongoing Education and Skill Development***

It is impossible to overestimate the importance of ongoing education and skill development in the fast-paced, constantly-changing labor market of today. Your path to financial freedom depends on your capacity to change, develop, and improve your skill set.

## *The Changing Nature of Employment*

There is a perpetual state of change in the work market. Rapid changes occur in customer preferences, industry trends, and technology. Things that were popular a few years ago could become outdated as new opportunities present themselves.

## The Significance of Ongoing Education

1. **Relevance**: Lifelong learning guarantees that you stay competitive and relevant in your industry. It enables you to stay current with changes and improvements in the business.

2. **Professional Growth**: Knowledge and abilities are essential for advancing one's career. You raise your chances of

promotions and higher-paying prospects by consistently honing your skills.

3. **Resilience**: Adapting to change is an essential talent. Ongoing education gives you the adaptability needed to handle job changes, whether they come about voluntarily or as a result of outside circumstances.

**Methods for Ongoing Education and Talent Acquisition**

1. **Virtual Education:** There are a plethora of online resources and courses available on the internet covering almost any topic. Resources such as Coursera, edX, and LinkedIn Learning offer chances to learn new skills or hone current ones.

2.**Graduation**: Obtaining certificates accepted by the business might greatly improve your job prospects. These certifications attest to your proficiency in the field and commitment to it.

3. **Career Advancement:** Participate in industry-related conferences, workshops, and seminars. These gatherings offer chances for networking and firsthand knowledge of current trends.

4. **Guest Leadership**: Look for advisors or mentors who can help you with your career. They can share their experiences, provide insightful advice, and encourage you on your learning path.

5. **Research and Reading**: Read books, research reports, and trade periodicals on a regular basis. This might assist you in keeping up with new concepts and trends in the market.

6. **Trials and error:** Apply the knowledge you have gained. You can gain important insights and expand your skill set by experimenting. Take risks, try new things, and learn from your mistakes as well as your accomplishments.

*A Mindset of Lifelong Learning*

Adopt a philosophy of lifelong learning. Understand that learning never ends, it never stops when you attend formal education. Develop an insatiable appetite for knowledge and inquiry. Rather than seeing impediments, see setbacks as chances for personal development.

You'll boost your potential income as well as your ability to adapt and bounce back from change if you make lifelong learning and skill development a priority in your career.

*Evan M. Dane*

Your continuous dedication to bettering yourself will be a valuable asset as you work toward financial freedom. We'll look at more tips to help you progress in your financial journey in the upcoming chapters.

## The Power of Investing

T he key to accumulating wealth and reaching financial independence is investing. We will give you an overview of the world of investing in this chapter, including stocks, bonds, and real estate. Gaining wealth over time requires knowing these asset classes and knowing how to invest your money.

## *Financial Independence via Investing*

The key to financial independence is learning to manage your money so that it works for you rather than just for you. Investing is a useful strategy that can help you grow your money faster than inflation and accumulate a sizable nest egg. Let's investigate the main investing paths.

## Equities

- **Explaining Stocks:** Stocks are a symbol of ownership in a business. Upon purchasing stocks, you become a shareholder and are entitled to the assets and profits of the business.
- **Roop for Development**: Historically, stocks have presented the best chance for long-term growth. Capital gains and dividends are available to you if you invest in profitable, well-managed businesses.
- **Dangers**: The value of stocks might change and they are vulnerable to market fluctuations. Spreading the risk in your stock portfolio requires diversification.

**Credits**

- **Bonds**: First, what are bonds? Debt instruments issued by corporations, governments, or other organizations are known as bonds. Purchasing a bond is akin to giving the issuer money in return for consistent interest payments and the principal repayment upon maturity.

- **Revenue and Steadiness**: Bonds are thought to be more stable than equities and are renowned for paying interest on a regular basis. They are frequently employed to produce steady cash flow.

- **Dangers**: The quality of the issuer's credit and fluctuations in interest rates might affect bond investments. It's critical to comprehend bond issuers' creditworthiness.

## A Property

- **Real Estate Investment:** Investing in real estate entails buying homes, businesses, or rental properties with the goal of increasing the value of the investment or earning rental revenue.

- **Income and Tangibility:** One tangible benefit of real estate investing is that you become the owner of a physical asset. Real estate properties can generate a consistent flow of cash flow through rental income.

- **Management and Maintenance:** Taking care of tenants and maintaining real estate properties calls for proactive management.

**Secularization**

One of the most important aspects of risk management is portfolio diversification. Investing in a variety of asset classes, such as bonds, real estate, and stocks, can lower risk and increase possible rewards.

**Compound Interest and Time**

Time is one of the most powerful weapons in investing. Your money might compound more the longer you invest. Compound interest speeds up the growth of your wealth by enabling your earnings to generate new earnings.

**Risk Acceptance and Objectives**

Your financial objectives and risk tolerance should be in line with your investment strategy. You may be able to take on more risk for maybe greater benefits if you have a longer time horizon. A more cautious strategy can be suitable if your objective is short-term.

Gaining an understanding of the principles of investing is essential as you move closer to financial independence. You may take use of the potential of investments to create wealth and get closer to your financial objectives by distributing your funds sensibly among stocks, bonds, real estate, and other assets. We'll look at investing techniques and approaches to safeguard your financial future in the next chapters.

### *Highlighting the Significance of Compound Interest and Extended Investment Approaches*

Few ideas are as influential in the world of finance as compound interest. You may get to financial independence much faster if you embrace long-term investing tactics and understand its importance.

**Compound Interest's Magic**

The increase in an investment's profits over time is known as compound interest. It's the idea of receiving interest on the interest you've already earned in addition to your initial investment. The secret to accumulating wealth is to take advantage of compound interest.

Here's why it matters:

1. **Exponential Growth**: Compound interest causes your investments to expand exponentially. Your earnings compound over time, resulting in a significant accumulation of wealth.

2. **Time Is On Your Side**: The impact of compound interest becomes more noticeable

the longer you leave your investments to grow. When it comes to creating substantial wealth, time is of the essence.

3. **Risk Mitigation**: You can lessen the effects of short-term volatility by investing for the long term and riding out market changes.

## Investment Strategies for the Long Term

1. **Go Earlier:** When you start early, compound interest has the most potential. Over time, even modest additions to your investments might yield substantial growth.

2. **Timely and Reliable Assistance:** Continually add to your investing portfolio. Compound interest can be fully utilized if you are consistent.

3. **Diversification**: To spread risk, spread your investments among a variety of asset

classes. This improves long-term stability and lessens the effects of market swings.

4. **Patience and Discipline:** Adhere to your investing plan and refrain from acting on impulse in response to transient market swings.

5. **Reinvest Dividends:** To maximize the benefits of compound interest, reinvested dividends or interest you earn from your investments.

## *A Practical Illustration*

Let's look at a straightforward example to show you the value of compound interest:

Let's say you deposit $10,000 into an account with a 7% yearly interest rate. One year from now, you will have $10,700. You make 7% on the first $10,000 and an extra 7% on the $700 you made the year before in the second year. Your money will continue to rise quicker each year as this cycle continues. Your $10,000 starting investment will have increased to almost $19,672 after ten years, almost doubling your money.

When this investment horizon is extended to 20, 30, or even 40 years, just think of the effects. It's clear that compound interest works: the longer you invest, the bigger the growth.

## *Adopting a Long-Term Vision*

Investing for the long term and building money is a marathon, not a sprint. It calls for perseverance, self-control, and unwavering dedication to your financial objectives. You put yourself on the road to financial freedom by turning to compound interest as your ally and adopting a long-term investing strategy.

# Financial Planning for Millennials

L ike any generation, millennials have their own set of financial requirements, objectives, and difficulties. This chapter will assist you in establishing a financial plan that supports the goals and lifestyles of millennials and will lead you on the road to financial freedom.

## *Understanding the Financial Reality of Millennials*

Factors such as student loan debt, the gig economy's growth, and a predilection for experiences above material goods are frequently used to define millennials. A customized financial plan can be informed by acknowledging these elements.

## Developing a Financial Plan with a Millennial Focus

**1. How to Handle Student Loans**: A major financial burden for a large number of millennials is student loan debt. Give top priority to coming up with a repayment strategy, taking into account refinancing and income-driven repayment plans.

2. **Reservations for Events**: Experiences are a higher priority for millennials than

material goods. Set aside money for experiences like travel and adventure, but make sure you're also saving and investing for the future.

3. **Flexible revenue:** Remote employment and the gig economy have increased the erratic nature of revenue sources. Include flexibility in your budget to account for changes in your revenue.

4. **Credit Emergency:** Keep a sizable emergency fund on hand because income in the gig economy might be irregular or erratic. Having a safety net for unforeseen costs is essential.

5. **Investment and Technology**: Adopt technology in order to make investments. Make use of platforms and apps that facilitate easy and convenient investing.

6. **Responsibility to Society:** Investments that are in line with millennials' social and environmental ideals are frequently valued by them. Investigate socially conscious and sustainable investment opportunities.

## *Short-Term and Long-Term Goal Balancing*

Younger generations often struggle to strike a balance between short-term needs and long-term financial goals. A balanced financial strategy that takes into account both short- and long-term objectives is crucial.

1. **Clear Goals:** Establish your financial objectives, encompassing both long-term and short-term goals (e.g., retirement and wealth accumulation), such as travel or property ownership.

2. **Cost Planning:** Make a budget that includes funds for both immediate gratification and long-term savings. In your budget, give savings first priority.

3. **Systematic Costs:** Establish automated transfers to achieve both immediate and long-term objectives. This makes sure you always set aside money for both.

4. **examine and Adjust**: As your objectives and situation change, periodically examine your financial plan and make the required modifications.

### *Advice and Education on Finance*

If you want to successfully manage the complicated world of finance, think about getting financial guidance and education that fits your millennial lifestyle. Make use of financial blogs, podcasts, and internet resources. You may also want to speak with financial consultants who are aware of your particular situation.

Understanding your generation's particular circumstances and financial objectives is essential to successful financial planning for millennials. Making a financial plan that fits your goals and way of life will allow you to take confident steps toward financial freedom. We'll look at sophisticated ways to increase your money and safeguard your financial future in the upcoming chapters.

*Evan M. Dane*

## *Addressing Millennials' Common Financial Challenges*

A distinct set of financial obstacles that millennials must overcome may hinder their path to financial freedom. A solid financial strategy must take these issues into consideration and be addressed. These are a few of the most typical financial obstacles that millennials encounter:

1. **Debt from student loans:**For many millennials, student loans are a major financial burden. Numerous people have substantial student loan debt as a result of high tuition fees and the requirement for higher degrees in today's employment market. To tackle this obstacle, a blend of tactics is needed:

- **payback Plans**: Look into income-driven payback schedules that correspond to your income.

- **Refinancing**: To obtain a reduced interest rate, consider refinancing your debts.

- **Budgeting**: Set aside money in your budget for loan payments, but don't forget to save for other financial objectives.

## 2. Income from Gig Economy:

Although the gig economy's growth has brought freedom, it can also lead to unpredictable revenue. It's critical to control this variability:

- **Emergency reserve**: Establish a sizable emergency reserve in order to pay unforeseen costs during difficult times.

- **Budget Flexibility**: Make a budget that is adaptable to changes in revenue.

- **Additional revenue Streams:** To augment your gig revenue, look into side projects or part-time work.

**3. Rental Prices:**

Rising urban housing costs can make it difficult for millennials to save money for other objectives. Among the solutions are:

- **Budget Wisely** :Be mindful of housing expenses and take co-living or roommate choices into consideration.

- **Alternate Locations**:Seek out reasonably priced neighborhoods with more inexpensive houses.

- **Realistic Homeownership**: Since becoming a homeowner may need significant savings and preparation, approach the process with a long-term outlook.

**4. Savings for Retirement:**

Sometimes, millennials value experiences over long-term savings. Experiences are important, but retirement savings are just as important:

❖ **Employer Plans**: If your employer matches contributions, make the most of your contributions to employer-sponsored retirement plans, such as 403(b)s or 401(k)s.

❖ **Roth IRAs**:Because they allow for tax-free withdrawals in retirement, you might choose to open one.

❖ **Automate Savings:** To make saving easy, set up automatic payments to retirement accounts.

## 5. Knowledge of Finances:

A large number of millennials lack basic financial literacy. Take up this task by:

★ **Self-Education**: Devote time to studying personal finance using online resources, podcasts, and books.

★ **Expert Advice:**To develop a customized financial plan, think about collaborating with a financial advisor.

## 6. Handling Debt:

High-interest loans and credit card debt can be costly traps. Among the strategies are:

➢ **Payback Plans for Debt:** Give high-interest debt priority when it comes to payback.

> **Budget Discipline**: Create a disciplined spending plan to stop the creation of new debt.

For millennials seeking financial independence, comprehending these typical obstacles and putting solutions in place is crucial. By being proactive in overcoming these obstacles, you may create a solid financial future for yourself.

# Realizing Entrepreneurial Dreams

The path to financial freedom for millennials who want to start their own business may be different. The realm of entrepreneurship is explored in this chapter, along with how it might lead to financial independence.

## *Business and Economic Self-Sufficiency*

There are few options as unique as entrepreneurship to achieve financial independence and freedom. It enables you to start your own company, take charge of your financial future, and maybe amass considerable riches.

**Investigating Business Concepts**

**1. Redundant Initiatives:**Begin with your hobbies and passions. What's your favorite thing to make or do? Businesses inspired by passion frequently have a better chance of succeeding.

**2. Identifying Market Needs**: Look into gaps and needs in the market. Is there an issue that has to be resolved? Are there any goods or services you can provide that meet these needs?

**3. Innovation**: Examine novel concepts and methods. What distinguishes your company from rivals? In what way can you offer a special value proposition?

**4.Market Analysis**: To comprehend your target market, the competitors, and market trends, conduct in-depth market research. Your company plan will be informed by this data.

**Creating Your Business Strategy**

Entrepreneurial success requires a well-organized business plan:

1. **Mission and Vision**: Specify the goals, principles, and long-term outlook for your company.

2. **Market Strategy:** Describe your target audience, your marketing approaches, and your goals for acquiring new clients.

3. **Financial Projections**: Make accurate financial estimates that account for beginning costs, income, and outlays.

4.**Operational Plan:** Describe your company's daily activities, including staffing, logistical, and technological needs.

**Supporting Your Business**

It can be difficult to get the first money you need for your business endeavor. Think about these choices:

1. Bootstrapping: Financing your company on your own with money from your present work and personal savings.

2. **crowdsourcing**: Using platforms for crowdsourcing to collect money from a big number of backers.

3. **Venture Capital and Angel Investors:** Seeking investors who are prepared to contribute funds in return for shares in your company.

4. **Small Business Loans**:Researching bank or lending institution small business loans.

**Risk Management**

Risks are part and parcel of being an entrepreneur. Controlling these hazards is crucial:

1. **Financial Cushion:** Establish a cushion of cash to pay for personal needs in tight times.

2. **Insurance**: To guard against unforeseen liabilities, think about getting company insurance.

3. **Ongoing Education:** Make an investment in your knowledge and abilities to adjust to evolving corporate landscapes.

4. **Mentorship**: Seek counsel from mentors or seasoned business owners who can provide knowledge and direction.

## Changing and Expanding

Being an entrepreneur is a continuous process. Think about these ideas for scaling and changing as your business expands:

1. **Employing:** As your company grows, you should think about outsourcing work or

recruiting more staff to keep up with demand.

**2. Technology:** Utilize technology to improve your online visibility and expedite processes.

**3. Marketing and Branding**: To remain competitive in the market, make constant improvements to your marketing and branding plans.

The path of entrepreneurship demands passion, tenacity, and a readiness to accept measured risks. It provides the chance to become financially independent and realize your aspirations.

Of course, those wishing to start their own business can find inspiration and insightful information in the tales of prosperous millennial entrepreneurs. Here are quick summaries of a few well-known millennial business owners:

*1. Mark Zuckerberg, Facebook's co-founder and CEO*

Among the most well-known millennial businesspeople is Mark Zuckerberg. While attending Harvard University, he co-founded Facebook, the largest social media network in the world, in 2004. Facebook has expanded into a multinational digital behemoth under his direction, connecting billions of users and purchasing firms like Instagram and WhatsApp.

*2. Snap Inc. (Snapchat) CEO and co-founder Evan Spiegel*

While still a Stanford University student in 2011, Evan Spiegel co-founded Snapchat. Snapchat, a well-known social media site, is recognized for its disappearing photo and video communications. Spiegel's success shows how creative concepts may upend established markets.

## 3. *Airbnb CEO and Co-Founder Brian Chesky*

In 2008, Brian Chesky and his fellow founders launched Airbnb. The website, which lets users rent out their houses to vacationers, has gained international acclaim. The sharing economy is powerful and has the capacity to upend established sectors, as demonstrated by Chesky's entrepreneurial journey.

## 4. *Kylie Jenner, Kylie Cosmetics' creator*

Member of the Kardashian-Jenner family, Kylie Jenner, introduced her cosmetics line, Kylie Cosmetics, in 2015. She used her social media presence and personal brand to develop a thriving cosmetics empire, highlighting the value of personal branding and leveraging one's skills.

**5. Ben Silbermann, Pinterest's co-founder and CEO**

Ben Silbermann was a co-founder of Pinterest, a website that lets people find and share ideas via photos, back in 2010. Millions of users now rely on Pinterest as a great source of inspiration, demonstrating the potential of specialized social media platforms.

**6. Melanie Perkins, Canva's CEO and co-founder**

In 2013, Melanie Perkins co-founded Canva, a graphic design platform that has enabled millions of users to access and democratize design tools. Her entrepreneurial career serves as an example of the value of meeting

*Evan M. Dane*

unmet needs and streamlining difficult activities.

These young business owners come from a variety of industries and backgrounds, but they all have a few things in common, like risk-taking, inventiveness, and tenacity. Aspiring business owners hoping to write their own success tales can draw inspiration and important lessons from their experiences.

# Part III

# Risk Management, Mindset, and Future Planning

## Navigating Financial Risks

A chieving financial independence involves more than just accumulating riches; it also entails safeguarding the hard-earned assets.

*Comprehending Risks Related to Money*

Uncertainties abound in life, and there are many different kinds of financial risk. In order to safeguard your financial stability, it is imperative that you recognize and reduce these risks. The following list of typical financial risks:

1. **Medical Expenses**: One may have to bear a heavy financial strain from medical bills. Costs that you must pay out of pocket could still exist even if you have a decent health plan.

2. **Responsibility and Property**:Insurance for your house and vehicle can protect your possessions in case of harm, theft, or collisions. Additionally, liability insurance shields you against court cases.

3. **Income Loss:** Unexpected unemployment or a disability may cause a large drop in income.

4.**Investment Hazards:** There is a risk associated with investing: market volatility. Your investment portfolio may be impacted by a stock market decline.

5. **Life and Disability**: It's important to protect your family's finances in the event that you pass away too soon or become disabled.

**Why Insurance Is Important**

One essential tool for controlling financial risks is insurance. It offers a safety net to shield your family, finances, and possessions. The following are some essential insurance kinds to think about:

1.**Medical Insurance:** It is essential to have sufficient health coverage. It guarantees you obtain the appropriate medical care and assists you with controlling medical costs.

2. **Home and Auto Insurance**: These policies guard against loss or damage to your goods and vehicles. Auto insurance with liability coverage also protects against court cases.

3. **Disability Insurance:** In the event that a disability prevents you from working, this insurance replaces your lost income.

4. **Terminology**: In the event of your death, life insurance offers your loved ones financial stability. Both short-term and long-term financial demands can be met by it.

5.**Umbrella Insurance**: Beyond the limitations of your previous insurance plans, umbrella insurance provides an additional layer of liability protection.

**Strategies for Risk Management**

Although insurance is an essential part of risk management, you should also think about the following alternative tactics:

1. **Emergency Fund:**Keep an emergency fund on hand to pay for unforeseen costs, such house repairs or medical expenditures.

2. **Investment Diversification:** To reduce market risks, diversify your portfolio of investments. Diverse asset types can aid in risk distribution.

3. **Estate Planning:**Take into account estate planning to guarantee that your assets are allocated in accordance with your desires and to reduce estate taxes.

4. **Cost and Budgeting:**You can better absorb financial shocks and manage income changes by maintaining a regular savings schedule and well-organized budget.

5. **Legal Protections:** Seek legal advice from experts to draft trusts, powers of attorney, and wills that safeguard your interests.

**Timely Evaluations**

It's critical to regularly examine your risk management techniques and insurance coverage as your circumstances change in life. Changes in your life circumstances, including getting married, having kids, or starting a new career, can need adjusting your risk management and insurance policies.

Achieving financial independence entails protecting your capital from unanticipated threats in addition to increasing it. You're securing your financial future by realizing the value of insurance and putting risk management techniques into practice.

## Methods for Safeguarding Resources and Wealth

It is just as important to protect and preserve your wealth and possessions as it is to accumulate them. Here are some tips for successfully safeguarding the accomplishments of your hard work:

### 1. Planning an Estate:

While lowering inheritance taxes, careful estate planning guarantees that your assets are allocated in the way you have specified. Think about the following components:

→ **Wills:**A will specify the distribution of your assets upon your death.

→ **Trusts**: Unlike wills, trusts allow for more flexibility in wealth management and distribution while requiring less public scrutiny.

→ **Powers of Attorney**: Designate people to handle financial and health-related decisions in the event that you become incapacitated.

→ **Beneficiary Designations**: Make that assets, such as retirement accounts and life insurance policies, go to the proper beneficiaries by keeping these updated.

2. **Diversification of Assets:**

One wise strategy to reduce risk in your investing portfolio is to diversify it. You lessen the effect of market swings by distributing your assets among a variety of investment kinds. A variety of equities, bonds, properties, and other asset classes are included in this.

3. **Savings Account**:

Keeping an emergency fund up to date is essential to protecting your assets. Savings that are easily available can help you pay for unforeseen costs like house repairs or medical bills without diminishing your investment portfolio.

**4. Lawful Defenses:**

To safeguard your assets from a variety of risks, such as lawsuits or creditor claims, get legal counsel. Trusts for the preservation of assets and thoughtfully designed corporate structures are examples of strategies.

**5. Frequent Evaluations:**

Your asset protection measures should adapt to changes in your life circumstances. Make sure your insurance policy, estate planning paperwork, and general financial strategy are still in line with your objectives and needs by reviewing them on a regular basis.

## 6. Handling Risk:

Reduce risks by using prudent planning and risk-management techniques. Refrain from subjecting your assets to needless risk and think about implementing risk management techniques in your commercial endeavors.

## 7. Security and Privacy:

Safeguarding your financial information is just as important as protecting your assets in the digital era. When sharing important information, encrypt it, create strong passwords, and keep an eye on your accounts for any unusual behavior.

Preserving your wealth and assets is a continuous process that needs careful thought and preparation. You can protect your money and financial stability for you and your loved ones by putting these strategies into practice.

# Mindset and Motivation

A valuable weapon in your quest for financial success is your thinking. look at how having a positive outlook might help you reach your financial objectives and maintain motivation along the way.

## The Influence of an Upbeat Attitude

On your journey to financial freedom, having a positive outlook can make all the difference. Why it matters is as follows:

1. **Hardiness**: Having an optimistic outlook gives you the fortitude to bounce back from setbacks and carry on. It enables you to see obstacles as chances for development.

2. **Center**: You concentrate harder on your objectives when your mind is concentrated on success. There is less chance of you becoming sidetracked by transient temptations.

3. **Solving Problems**:Thinking positively inspires original problem-solving. You

approach problems with a can-do mentality and solve problems more quickly.

4.**Improved Decision-Making**: Making decisions with clarity and reason is facilitated by positivity. You are able to objectively consider your options and make decisions that support your objectives.

5. **Social Media:** Positivity is a powerful tool for developing a solid professional network. People are drawn to people who radiate enthusiasm and confidence.

**Developing an Upbeat Attitude**

The following techniques can help you develop and preserve a happy outlook:

1. **Establish Specific Goals**: Clearly state your financial objectives. Setting clear goals helps you feel purposeful and directed.

2. **Display of Data:** Continually envision your achievement. Make a mental image of yourself accomplishing your objectives.

3. **Positive Affirmations:** Reaffirm your self-belief and your success vision by using positive affirmations.

4. **Ongoing Education**: Adopt a growth mentality. Acknowledge that learning and developing oneself are constant activities.

5. **Empathy with Oneself**: Treat yourself with love, especially when you experience failures. Show yourself the same consideration that you would a friend.

6. **Surround Yourself with Positive People**: Assemble a positive and goal-oriented circle of people around you.

**Survival and Determination**

The impetus behind taking action to accomplish your goals is called motivation. This is how to maintain motivation:

1. **Discover Your Why**:Recognize your motivations for wanting to become financially independent. Your "why" serves as an effective catalyst.

2. **Break Down Your Goals:** Break down your objectives into more doable, smaller steps. This keeps motivation high and makes them more attainable.

3. **Honor Milestones:** Honor your accomplishments along the route. Recognizing your advancements might increase your drive.

4. **Accountability**: Talk to someone who can help you stay accountable about your goals.

5. **Consistency**: Establish daily or weekly schedules that help you stay organized and focused.

6. **Adjust to Difficulties**: There will be obstacles and disappointments along the way. Adapt and keep going forward rather than giving up.

7. **Visualization**: To boost your motivation, use visualization techniques to imagine yourself achieving your objectives.

You may gradually build and reinforce your motivation and thinking. A meaningful life and financial success are within your reach if you maintain motivation and cultivate a good outlook.

Strategies to help you remain inspired and unwavering in your pursuit of financial success:

1. **Make Specific, Meaningful Objectives**: A strong motivator is having financial goals that are clear and significant. Goals that are both personally meaningful and well-defined increase the likelihood of sustained commitment. Put your objectives down on paper, divide them into more manageable chunks, and go over them frequently.

2. **Envision Your Achievement:**
A powerful strategy employed by many prosperous people is visualization. Visualize your goals coming to pass on a regular basis. Imagine the lifestyle and freedom that come with achieving your desired level of financial independence. This kind of mental visualization helps increase willpower and drive.

3. **Make a Board of Visions:**

A vision board is a printed or digital collage of pictures and text that you can use to express your aspirations and goals. It might help you stay motivated by acting as a visual reminder of your goals.

**4. Divide Objectives Into More Manageable Steps:**

Break down your bigger financial objectives into more doable, smaller steps. This lessens the sensation of overwhelm on the road and gives each milestone a sense of accomplishment. Celebrate your victories along the road to keep yourself motivated.

**5. Take Responsibility:**

Tell a mentor, family member, or trusted friend about your goals so they can help you stay on track. You can keep on track by checking in with someone who supports your goals on a regular basis.

## 6.Set deadlines:

Set attainable deadlines for your financial objectives. Setting deadlines makes you feel pressed for time and motivates you to act consistently.

## 7. Give Yourself a Treat:

Create a system of rewards for reaching your objectives and benchmarks. Honoring your accomplishments can strengthen your resolve to succeed financially and increase drive.

## 8. Keep Things Uniform:

Establish weekly or daily schedules that support your objectives. Maintaining your motivation and persistence requires consistency. Include routine financial duties and habits in your daily routine.

## 9.Adjust to Difficulties:

Every journey has its share of obstacles and failures. Consider them as opportunities to learn and develop rather than as obstacles to overcome. When faced with challenges, modify your strategy and keep going.

10.. **Look for Motivation:**

Read biographies of successful financial people in books, in films, or on podcasts. Gaining inspiration and insightful knowledge might come from studying the experiences of others.

11.**Exercise Self-Compassion:**

Treat yourself with love, especially when you experience failures. Show yourself the same consideration that you would a friend. Acknowledge that making errors is normal and that perfection is not required.

12. **Keep an Environment That Is Supportive:**

Be in the company of people who encourage you to pursue your aspirations. An setting that is upbeat and encouraging can give you the boost you need to stay inspired.

Keep in mind that it's common for motivation to fluctuate. By putting these strategies into practice and incorporating them into your daily routine, you may improve your drive and perseverance as you work toward financial success.

# Preparing for the Future

S ecuring your financial future is just as important as focusing on the now while achieving financial freedom.

*The Value of Forward Planning*

It's simple for millennials pursuing financial freedom to concentrate on short-term objectives and experiences. But it's also important to think about your long-term financial health. Reasons it's important to plan ahead:

1. **Safety in Retirement:** Retirement planning guarantees you may enjoy your latter years without worrying about money. It gives you the flexibility to follow your passions and interests.

2. **Preservation of Wealth and Legacy**:Preserving the riches you have amassed to give to charitable organizations or future generations is another aspect of planning for the future.

3. **Unexpected Costs:** Things happen in life. Making plans for the future helps you be ready for unforeseen medical costs, legal issues, or other financial difficulties.

4.**Planning for Retirement:** A vital component of preparing for the future is retirement planning.

i. Go Earlier:The more time you give your money to grow, the earlier you start saving for retirement. Benefit from employer-sponsored programs such as IRAs and 401(k)s.

ii. Set Specific Objectives:Ascertain your ideal retirement lifestyle and project your future spending.

iii.Maximize Contributions: If your employer matches your contribution, add as much as you can to your retirement accounts.

iv.Diversify Investments: Risk can be reduced by diversifying the investments in your retirement account. Balance can be achieved by combining stocks, bonds, and other assets.

v.Review Your Plan Often:Make sure your retirement plan is still in line with your objectives and financial circumstances by reviewing it on a regular basis.

**Preservation of Wealth**

Protecting your assets and making sure they last for future generations or causes you care about is what wealth preservation is all about. Among the strategies are:

- Real Estate: Make a thorough estate plan that includes powers of attorney, trusts, and wills. Your assets will be allocated in accordance with your intentions thanks to this strategy.

- Tax Planning: Learn about tax-saving options to reduce estate taxes and safeguard your assets.

- Insurance: To safeguard the financial stability of your family, make sure you have the appropriate insurance, including life insurance.

- Legal Protections: Put legal safeguards in place to protect your assets from future debts or lawsuits.

**Halving Current and Future Objectives**

Many millennials struggle to strike a balance between planning for the future and enjoying the moment. Finding a balance between securing your financial future and enjoying life today is crucial.

Think about taking these important actions:

❖ Budget Wisely: While maintaining your current standard of living, set aside a percentage of your salary for retirement savings and wealth preservation.

❖ Automate Savings:To guarantee consistency in future savings, set up automatic contributions to retirement accounts.

❖ Examine and Adjust: As your goals and circumstances change, periodically examine your financial plan and make any required adjustments.

Making a plan for the future is an investment in your mental and financial stability. You're taking action to safeguard your financial future, guaranteeing that you may enjoy the rewards of your hard work and leave a lasting legacy, by thinking about retirement planning and wealth preservation.

## *Talking About Creating Generational Wealth and Estate Planning*

Developing generational wealth is more than just increasing your holdings; it's also about making sure they last and offer your offspring stability. Planning for the future is an essential part of this process.

## A Basis for Generational Wealth: Estate Planning

The act of setting up your financial affairs in order to guarantee that your assets are allocated in accordance with your final intentions is known as estate planning. It's essential to creating wealth for future generations for a number of reasons.

1. Wealth Transfer:With estate planning, you can manage the way your wealth is passed down to the following generation. It is up to you to decide what gets to whom, when, and under what circumstances.

2. Cutting Down on Taxes: You can ensure that your successors receive a larger portion of your fortune by minimizing estate and inheritance taxes through careful estate planning.

3. Safeguarding Resources:It provides asset protection, insulating your assets from future liabilities or legal demands.

4. Smooth Transition:A well-crafted estate plan makes the transfer of assets easier, lessening the strain on your heirs and lowering the possibility of disagreements.

**Important Aspects of Estate Planning**

1. Assent:A legal document known as a will specifies your preferences for how you distribute assets and provide for any dependents. Making sure your assets go where you want them to is crucial.

2. Beliefs:Trusts provide you greater control over the distribution of your assets by letting you decide how and when recipients will get their inheritance. They may also provide secrecy and probate protection.

3. Powers of Attorney: In the event of your incapacity, these legal documents name someone to handle financial and medical decisions on your behalf.

4. Healthcare Directives:These express your preferences for medical care in the event that you are unable to make decisions for yourself.

5. Designations of Beneficiaries:For assets like retirement accounts and life insurance policies, be sure these designations are current. Probate is avoided, and the designated beneficiaries receive them immediately.

**Creating Wealth Across Generations**

Creating generational wealth entails expanding your assets over time in addition to safeguarding them. Here's how to work toward this objective:

1. Investment Strategies: Make prudent investments to gradually increase your wealth. To optimize results, diversify your holdings and take long-term strategy into account.

2. Learning: Promote appropriate financial management and financial literacy in your

household. Instruct students on budgeting, investing, and saving.

3. Entrepreneurship and Business:Think about transferring your firm to the following generation if you are the owner. As an alternative, support your family's business endeavors.

4. Philanthropy: Include donations to charities in your budget. Giving back to the community and fostering a sense of purpose can be achieved through philanthropy, which can be a vital component of generational wealth.

5. Interaction: It's critical to communicate with your heirs in an honest and open manner. Talk about your plans for generational wealth, values, and financial goals. Promote stewardship and financial responsibility.

6. Seek Professional Guidance: To make sure your wealth transfer plan is properly structured and tax-efficient, confer with estate planning specialists and financial advisors.

Effective estate planning and generating wealth for future generations go hand in hand. You may preserve your financial legacy for future generations by drafting a careful estate plan and encouraging an entrepreneurial and responsible financial culture within your family.

# Resources for Millennials

F or millennials who are working toward financial independence, access to worthwhile resources and continued education are essential. A carefully selected selection of tools, websites, and publications to aid in your financial journey is provided in this chapter.

**Online Resources and Websites**

1. Mint:An easy-to-use, free budgeting app that assists you in keeping tabs on your

spending and making a customized financial plan.

2. Investopedia:*An excellent source of information on concepts, vocabulary, and investment tactics related to finance.

3. Khan University: provides free classes on a variety of financial subjects, such as taxes, retirement planning, and investing.

4. The Motley Fool: An excellent resource for stock market research, investing guidance, and extensive instructional materials.

5. NerdWallet: Offers helpful tools, professional guidance, and comparisons of financial products for managing your finances.

**Looking for Financial Communities and Mentors**

*Evan M. Dane*

You don't have to go it alone on the road to financial independence. In actuality, interacting with financial networks and asking mentors for advice and assistance may really improve things. This is the reason it matters:

1. Taking Experience to Heart:Mentors can share their experiences and offer priceless insights, particularly if they have achieved financial success. They can provide advice on your path since they have experienced the difficulties.

2. Accountability and Motivation:Mentors can help you stay motivated and hold you responsible for reaching your financial objectives. One of the most potent motivators is the knowledge that someone is observing your progress.

3. Networking Possibilities:Online or in-person financial communities offer networking chances. You may interact with people who share your interests, exchange stories, and gain knowledge from one another.

4. Resource Access: You can make better financial decisions by using the resources, tools, and knowledge that mentors and the financial community frequently have access to.

5. Help with Emotions:At times lonely and difficult, achieving financial freedom can be a journey. Financial communities and mentors provide understanding and emotional support.

**Seek Out Mentors:**

1. Look in Your Network: Begin by thinking about individuals in your current network who possess financial acumen or achievement. They might be acquaintances, coworkers, friends, or relatives.

2. Seek Out Professionals: Leaders in business, financial advice, or subject matter expertise can make great mentors. Do not be scared to ask them for help.

3. Online Communities: Financial independence-focused social media organizations and online networks such as LinkedIn frequently have seasoned mentors eager to share their expertise.

4. Networking Events: To meet possible mentors, go to local conferences, seminars, and networking events in the financial sector.

**Becoming a Part of Financial Communities**

1. Internet forums: Online forums and groups such as Bogleheads, Reddit's r/personalfinance, and other financial subreddits provide a wealth of knowledge and a place to ask questions.

2. The use of social media: You can interact with financial professionals and enthusiasts through groups and communities on social media sites like Facebook, Twitter, and LinkedIn.

3. Groups for Meetups: Look for Meetup groups that are local finance in your region. They frequently host conferences, seminars, and talks regarding investing and personal finance.

4. Professional Organizations: Sign up for groups that support your objectives and areas of interest in finance.

5. Workshops and Conferences: Attend seminars on investing and financial independence to network with industry leaders and like-minded people.

Keep in mind that relationships in the financial world should be two-way while looking for mentors or joining communities. It's important to consider what you can offer them in addition to what you can get from them. As you move forward in your financial journey, be willing to share and give back.

Your journey to financial independence can be greatly accelerated by the support, information, and contacts you make, whether you choose to interact with financial communities or look for mentors. Keep in mind that the journey is about the experiences and connections you make along the way, not simply about getting to your destination.

# Acknowledgement

Writing a book is never something you do alone. It is the result of numerous people and resources coming together to provide support, direction, and inspiration. I want to express my sincere appreciation to everyone who has helped make this book a reality.

I want to start by sincerely thanking my family, whose constant support and faith in my vision have laid the groundwork for my road towards financial freedom. My never-ending source of motivation has been your love and support.

I am grateful to my mentors and financial advisors for sharing their knowledge, perspectives, and experiences. Your advice has been really helpful to me in understanding the complexities of wealth-building and in structuring the substance of this book.

I also want to thank all of the writers, bloggers, and thought leaders that I have come across in the personal finance and financial independence fields. Your writings have been a wealth of information, and I appreciate the aggregate knowledge you have imparted to the globe.

I appreciate your enthusiasm and support, friends and coworkers who have been my sounding board and inspiration. I've persevered through the highs and lows of this creative process because of your support.

I want to express my gratitude to all of the readers and students who have delved into the wide realm of personal finance and financial literacy. We are all inspired by your commitment to enhancing your financial situation.

# *NOTES*

*Evan M. Dane*

www.ingramcontent.com/pod-product-compliance
Lightning Source LLC
Chambersburg PA
CBHW072216290526
45794CB00004B/1762